WHEN CLERICS KILL

DRAMA

Kraftgriots

Also in the series (DRAMA)

WHEN CLERICS KILL

DRAMA

Shehu Sani

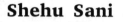

kraftgriots

Published by

Kraft Books Limited
6A Polytechnic Road, Sango, Ibadan
Box 22084, University of Ibadan Post Office
Ibadan, Oyo State, Nigeria
℡ 0803 348 2474, 0805 129 1191
E-mail: kraftbooks@yahoo.com

First published 2013

ISBN 978–978–918–084–4

= KRAFTGRIOTS =
(A literary imprint of Kraft Books Limited)

First printing, January 2013

DEDICATION

To all those persecuted or killed for their religious beliefs or ethnic identity or impaired as such.

ACKNOWLEDGEMENT

This is to acknowledge the patience of my family and the input of all those who edited and gave the play a stage meaning.

# AUTHOR'S NOTE

The play is about intolerance, about bigotry, about violence and about peace. It begins with disturbing views and enlightening conversation and graduates to a session of tension and orgy. It is about the influence and impact of religious leaders in the perception and conduct of a given society. The play is to submit for the audience the angle of their reasoning and justifications.

The play reveals the role played by various elements presented as characters in shaping, destroying or rescuing societies in the grip of hate and extremism. It presents all angles in their best of forms and stand. The play is a rendition of the occurrences in a given society as it affects women, youths and life in general. What do women think, what do the youths think, what is the thought of everyone and what becomes of everyone? How do housewives and the young people survive a society torn apart physically and spiritually? The play presents the spiritual, cultural and moral perception of Religionists and Theocrats. To the best way possible, they are crafted to speak on stage without denigrating the substance of their beliefs. All views are set on stage against opposing views and within the context and conflict of such views in a heterogeneous society. The play recognizes the rights of people to hold beliefs, the righteousness of peace and the futility of violence and compulsion.

A scene in the play deals with the exuberance of

young people and the vulnerability of their minds to go to the extreme. They converse about ideology, about politics, about religion and about the failed duty of the state to insure their future. Secularists confront religionists and religionists confront the state. Another scene also digs out the role of political leaders and the challenge of governance in crisis-ridden societies. It stages debates on balancing politics, human rights on the one hand and the imperative of restoring or maintaining law and order on the other. The play delves into the conduct of security personnel in crisis times, their arbitrariness and excessiveness. How they exploit and profit from emergency situations. The interrogation aspects of the play are to use the questions and answers provided to educate the audience. It is hoped that such a discourse will cast light on why some people say what they say and do what they do.

The play is written with the sole aim of promoting peace and motivating peace efforts in societies dislocated or paralyzed by wanton religious or ethnic violence. It is meant to inspire as well as to inculcate into the conscience of the society the spirit of love, tolerance and interreligious harmony. The play makes no pretence in its outright denunciation of hate and human rights violation committed in any guise and for any purpose. It propagates opposition to extremism and encourages people to reject fear and silence, and rise to the defence of freedom and fundamental rights. The play exposes the failure of governance and the causative factors of corruption, decadence, religious persecution and cruelty and criminality of the state apparatus that lead to desperate and virulent reactions from victims.

The play is not for entertainment. It is a literary contribution and intervention in the search for peace in a seemingly perpetually troubled world. In countries and communities where religion plays an important role in the lives of the inhabitants, clerics hold a special place in the hearts and minds of the people. They are viewed as a moral authority and a spiritual force. They are increasingly becoming more dependable in a world of fluctuating or failing political and economic theories. What they say and what they do matter. And when some of them with followers take the wrong path, the end is predictable. *When Clerics Kill* is about what happens when they choose not to conform to the principles of tolerance and coexistence.

# CHARACTERS

Martha John	} A Christian couple
Tani Sagir	} A Muslim couple
Steve Adam Rais Ibro	} Jobless graduates
Gambo	An employed graduate
Mahdi Saka Yakubu	} Undergraduates

Governor
Aide I
Aide II
Soldier
Police head
Police 1
Police 2
Commissioner
Ambassador
Ehud

Imam
Pastor
Sheikh Jabar   –   An Islamic extremist
Pastor Gatari   –   A Christain extremist
Panelist 1
Panelist 2
Panelist 3

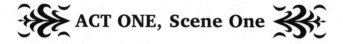

ACT ONE, Scene One

Early evening, a family compound with thatch-roofed houses. Three houses forming a circle with space at the middle. One of them is the kitchen. Children playing at the centre of the compound, Mr JOHN repairs and cleans his bicycle in front of one of the houses. MARTHA, his wife, is by his side, peeling some tubers of yam.

MARTHA: (*In a concerned tone.*) My dear, these days you appear so worried and restless and you are not the uxorious man I know. Have I done anything wrong or could someone have upset you?

JOHN: (*Turning to her.*) No, Dear. It's none of what you are saying.

MARTHA: Then what is it? I am very much disturbed seeing you in this mood.

JOHN: Well, Dear, I'm very much worried about the trend of things in this town.

MARTHA: (*Leaves the yam and turns fully to him.*) What trend and what happened?

JOHN: Some people are trying to dominate and dictate to us how to live our lives.

MARTHA: (*Casually.*) My dear, politics again. The last time you came here campaigning for the Councillor and now he is in the office and you are saying they are trying to dominate. What do you mean by that? (*Resumes the peeling of the yam.*)

JOHN: I'm not talking about the Councillor. Listen, I'm talking about these rebarbative settlers.

MARTHA: Who are the settlers?

JOHN: These settlers, Hausa, Muslim people.

MARTHA: Settlers? When did they become settlers? (*Takes the yam inside the kitchen and returns to her husband.*)

JOHN: Don't you know they are settlers?

MARTHA: How do you call people with whom we have lived for so long, even with our great-grandfathers settlers? I don't understand what you are trying to say.

JOHN: That was sufferance. It does not matter even if they are here for a thousand years. They are still settlers. We are the indigenous people here. This is where our ancestors are. These settlers came from the desert. They are Muslims, we are Christians. Know this, Woman.

MARTHA: (*Clapping her hands surprisingly.*) I am really surprised. Since we married I have never heard you talk like this. We live together with these people as one. We respect each other and now why this pestilent ...

JOHN: (*Tries to convince the wife, cuts.*) Hey! hey!! Stop this. Don't deceive yourself, these people hate us. They call us infidels or unbelievers. They took over our farmlands and built big houses and shops and ...

MARTHA: (*Cuts in.*) My dear, these thoughts of yours are strange to me. Since you started attending these meetings at the house of Pastor Gatari, I have not been comfortable. I never like that man and his sententious postulations and it's now clear to me that he is indoctrinating you.

JOHN: (*Casually*.) Well, whatever you can say, but for all I know, Gatari is an upright and intelligent man and all he is saying is true and enlightening to a recondite society of ours. For your knowledge, the meeting I attend in his house is for a new organization, Indigenous Peoples Forum, which we founded and he is the Chairman.

MARTHA: So, why the forum now and what's the use of such an organization?

JOHN: The forum is out to protect and preserve our Christian values and culture and to free us from the impending dominance of the Muslims. And to save our town from being Islamized. You will join us when we form the women's wing soon. We are out to defend our way of lives with pertinacity.

MARTHA: (*Calmly*.) My dear, you have to be careful and all of you in that group should be careful. Pastor Gatari has been living outside this town for over 20 years. Now he is back with these anarchist and annihilating ideas. We have been living in peace all this while with these Muslims. I'm warning you that what you people are doing will not free us from anything but will only create division within ourselves.

JOHN: You are just a woman, you won't understand. This group is indispensable for our survival. If we don't stand up to these people you will be shocked that they will swallow us all up soon. You should understand. These Muslims are not living in peace with us. They are just biding their time. They are people with a thirst for conquest.

MARTHA: My dear, your ideas are giving me headache and heartache. We have been living together for generations as neighbours. We go to the same market. Our children attend the same school. They come over here to celebrate Christmas and Easter with us. We go to their houses to celebrate their Eid Fitr and Eid El kabir. We share food and share farmlands.

JOHN: Don't deceive yourself and don't allow yourself to be deceived. This is our land. Muslims do not belong here. They are settlers. We are not the same. We are the landlords and they are tenants. A tenant cannot be equal to the landlord. Pastor Gatari has read out a verse in the Qur'an. It said that they should fight the infidels. And that infidels and Muslims can never be friends.

MARTHA: Now what do you people want to do? To drive away all the Muslims or what? You know that is impossible and a dangerous thought.

JOHN: Well, we will get there. Our position is either they have to live here on our terms or they will leave here on our terms.

MARTHA: My dear, perish this thought in the interest of peace and that of our children. Pastor Gatari is indeed a troublemaker. How could he come here and sell this kind of idea to you while his family don't live here?

JOHN: Look, it's not about Pastor Gatari. Look not on

the messenger but the message.

MARTHA: What message is there in this seed of hatred and trouble he is sowing?

JOHN: (*Abandons the bicycle.*) I'll list them for you and you will tell me whether they are true or false.

MARTHA: I am listening, number one.

JOHN: On Fridays in this town, the Muslims block all roads leading to their mosque area simply because they are praying. And anyone who tries to just pass by, they molest him or her.

MARTHA: Number two.

JOHN: They erected an illegal wall across the grave yard to separate the graves of their dead people from ours.

MARTHA: Number three.

JOHN: The Fulani herdsmen carelessly and arrogantly allow their cattle to feed on the crops of our farmers, damaging our farmland.

MARTHA: Four.

JOHN: They built a new abattoir, saying that they cannot slaughter their cattle where we slaughter our pigs.

MARTHA: Five.

JOHN: They have recently ordered all alcohol sellers to leave the market square. And some Muslim youths just three days ago beat up an owner of a restaurant they accused of selling beer in the market.

MARTHA: Six.

JOHN: Just yesternight, some Muslim youths entered

a hotel and beat up some women they accused of prostitution.

MARTHA: Seven.

JOHN: They instructed their children in school to start wearing hijab and stop wearing the school uniform recognized and approved by the Ministry of Education.

MARTHA: Eight.

JOHN: Can't you see what is happening in the general hospital, all the Muslim nurses are now wearing hijab and not the one approved by the Ministry of Health? (*Angrily.*) Now what have you got to say?

MARTHA: Well, I understand your points but I think all these issues can be addressed through dialogue and understanding and not through roguish means.

JOHN: What dialogue and what understanding?

MARTHA: First about their Friday prayer. You should understand that because of their sheer number, their mosque cannot contain them so they have to spread outside and they are done within an hour, so I don't see anything wrong with that.

JOHN: Two.

MARTHA: Erecting a fence and demarcating Christian graves from Muslim graves is also not a bad idea, after all they bury their people differently from the way we bury ours.

JOHN: Three.

MARTHA: As for the Fulani herdsmen, I believe it's the responsibility of government to create a grazing reserve that will solve this problem. Well, you know we cannot live without meat. We need them in as much as they need the farmers.

JOHN: Four.

MARTHA: Well if they don't eat pork and went ahead to build their own abattoir, fine, there is nothing wrong with that. You can choose not to eat their beef, too.

JOHN: Five.

MARTHA: My dear, you are a Christian, what is your own defending alcohol sellers? Does Christianity permit alcohol consumption? The way we criticize Muslims for their prohibitive stance on alcohol is as if our religion approves of it.

JOHN: Six.

MARTHA: Brothels are not churches and those prostitutes that were beaten by the Muslim youths are not representatives of Christianity. They are symbols of abhorrent sin which every genuine Christian must condemn. I don't think as a Christian you should lose your sleep if prostitutes are beaten. Except if you want to tell me that our religion approves of it. I believe you are neither a ponce nor a philanderer.

JOHN: Seven.

MARTHA: I actually do not know the reason why we Chrisitans should be so irritated about hijab worn by Muslims either in schools or hospitals. What is the difference between a hijab and the apparel worn by Mary the mother of Christ? It is insulting to Christianity to think that Christianity approves of its believers to expose their bodies while Muslims should cover theirs. I think decent dressing is an inherent part of Christianity. Women walking naked and parading themselves as Christians are simply desecrating themselves.

JOHN: I come to understand that your blind and ignorant hate for Pastor Gatari is preventing you from seeing the truth in what affects your life.

MARTHA: It's not about hating Gatari; it is about saving you and others from his misinformation. It's about saving our peace and togetherness from an impending doom such an idea can lead to.

JOHN: (*Resumes work on his bicycle.*) You are a woman. Your thoughts are shallow and narrow. You have no grasp of the situation at hand. All you want is for us to continue to placidly submit and surrender to these Muslims. If this town will go by your thoughts, we will one day wake up as slaves to the Muslims, in our very own town. (*Looks at his wife.*) If you see nothing wrong with this, all you are saying is that one day we should even accept Sharia law. They have even started agitating for Sharia law. I guess you will also defend them on that.

MARTHA: (*Defensively.*) Come on, Dear, I am not defending them. I'm simply pointing out to you the implication of all of these thoughts of yours. Recently I overheard them on the radio saying they want Sharia for themselves and not to be imposed on anyone. So what is wrong with that? How does that affect you? You need to understand that tolerance is your resistance in this town.

20

JOHN: (*Raises a finger at his wife and in a warning tone.*) Yes, they can have Sharia in other places but not on this land of my ancestors and church. Over my dead body. There is no use talking with you. (*Storms out, leaving a surprised look on the wife's face. Lights out.*)

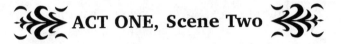

ACT ONE, Scene Two

SAGIR *and his wife* TANI *feed the family herd of sheep in the barn. They are young Muslims in the community.*

TANI: My dear, I saw the CD of Sheikh Jabbar's sermon or is it preaching you brought home and I listened to it all.

SAGIR: How did you find it?

TANI: Scary, ratty and his vision a phantasm!

SAGIR: What do you mean by "scary"?

TANI: (*Looks worried.*) I thought that man is a man of peace, but all he has been saying in his preaching is nothing but promoting hate, intolerance and fanning the embers of discord.

SAGIR: (*Casually.*) What is there about hate and intolerance?

TANI: He was just chapter by chapter attacking the Christians and saying so many discomforting things and in my view, that is not good for our kind of multireligious and multiethnic society. His utterances are solipsist.

SAGIR: Don't be so naïve. What is it that he said about the Christians that is not true?

TANI: Dear, you really seem to have been convinced by this psychopath, perhaps that is why you always attend his Tafsir.

SAGIR: As far as I'm concerned, all his arguments are

valid. The Christians in this town are infidels.

TANI: When did they start becoming infidels? Is it when Sheikh Jabbar started coming to this town to preach? How can you call them infidels, such good people we have been living together in peace with for generations?

SAGIR: (*Angrily*.) Yes, we have lived with them for generations but they still refer to us as settlers and they call themselves indigenes.

TANI: (*Persuasively*.) Oh, Dear, why are you so sentimental about that? I think you should be very careful with this Sheik Jabbar. He seems to be getting into your head. We are living in peace with the Christians, a preacher who came all the way from Kano must not come here and sow the seed of hate among us.

SAGIR: It's not about hate. It's about you being a Muslim and must live your life according to the Islamic injunctions as prescribed by the Sunnah of our revered Prophet Muhammad, peace and blessing of Allah be upon him.

TANI: But that is indeed the life we are living now. But I want you to understand that this town is multi-religious. It is not Mecca or Tehran. I mean, we have Muslims and Christians: we must tolerate each other in the interest of peace.

SAGIR: (*Angrily*.) Whether you call our town or country multireligious or multiethnic or secular, a Muslim must protect his identity and propagate his religion without hindrance. Any form of hindrance is a declaration of war against Islam and cannot be tolerated.

TANI: (*Comes closer to her husband.*) Now tell me, what is it that the Christians have done or are doing that you find disgusting? I'm really surprised by your fiery, disconnecting arguments. You were not like this before.

SAGIR: (*He holds her and they both sit down and continue.*) Yes, I was not like this but now I have seen the light. And I will tell you what is going on in this town. Obviously, there is a subversion against our religion.

TANI: I'm all ears.

SAGIR: One, if the Christians apply for permit to build their churches, it only takes few days for the state government to approve, but if it's Muslims, it takes years and most times they will even deny it.

TANI: Two.

SAGIR: Because every year we travel to Saudi Arabia for Hajj, an essential component of the pillar of our religion, they too decided to concoct a false pilgrimage by going to Israel, which is not an obligation. And there is nowhere in the Bible where Christians are told to go on a pilgrimage to Jerusalem. And worse of all, the state government will sponsor thousands of them and only allocate a fraction of that to the Muslims.

TANI: Three.

SAGIR: The government has given out licence for people to sell and drink alcohol even in areas inhabited by Muslims; and this cannot be.

TANI: Four.

SAGIR: See the proliferation of brothels in this town. Prostitutes have now taken over most streets. Gambling and all sorts of satanic activities by the Christians have become a common feature.

TANI: Five.

SAGIR: They have turned the abattoir into a place where they slaughter pigs and dogs for meat, it is unislamic to share such a place with them.

TANI: Six.

SAGIR: Christian women nowadays move about almost naked. Is this Christianity or simply sheer Satanism?

TANI: Seven.

SAGIR: Many Islamic preachers are nowadays denied preaching permit on the ground of security concerns while Christian evangelists are permitted to hold both day and night open air mass.

TANI: Eight.

SAGIR: Many of our Muslim Fulani heardsmen have reported that they are continuously facing harassment by Christian villagers around this town, and even most often their cows are seized by force. Is this an act of peace or togetherness?

TANI: Nine.

SAGIR: Look at the last local government elections, the Christian governor of this state refused to swear in the Muslim chairman and the councillors who won their elections. He instead imposed an administrator who is a Christian.

TANI: Ten.

SAGIR: All the major appointments in the state and local government system are given to the Christians. All the juicy contracts in this state go to the Christians. Before one Muslim graduate is given an employment, over ten Christians must have been employed. Even in fertilizer distribution to farmers by the government, they give priority to Christian farmers before Muslims.

TANI: Eleven.

SAGIR: (*Stands up in anger. Points a finger at his wife.*) Just think about those ten posers and ask yourself whether this kind of society of ours is not ripe for a holy war.

TANI: (*In a fearful tone.*) A jihad?

SAGIR: Yes, a jihad. Muslims are oppressed. We have to free ourselves. We can't continue to live in this kind of sinful and idolatrous society with a biased and luciferous governor defending his Christian brothers and spitting on us.

TANI: I think I beg to differ.

SAGIR: In what sense?

TANI: On most of those issues you raised.

SAGIR: Let me hear your reasons. (*Comes back to sit again.*)

TANI: From my own knowledge, the government only denies permit for erection of buildings in undesignated areas like public parks and walkways. I don't think it's right to request to build a mosque or any structure in places not included in the town master plan.

SAGIR: Two.

TANI: About the pilgrimage, what you also need to understand is that in other states of the federation where Muslims are the majority, the same rule applies; Christians are given marginal slots and Muslims are given the majority of the seats.

SAGIR: And tell me in the Bible where it is said that Christians should go to Jerusalem for pilgrimage.

TANI: I don't know about that.

SAGIR: OK, continue.

TANI: As for the Fulani herdsmen, I don't think it's fair for them to allow their cattle to feed on other people's farms. Even me, I don't think I should work hard to grow my crops in my farm just for a herdsman to carelessly allow his flocks to feed on my crops. And I wish to draw your attention to the fact that the Fulani have been having problems even with the Muslim farmers.

SAGIR: Go on.

TANI: As for the way the Christians dress, I don't think that should bother you. If we Muslims decide to cover ourselves, it's our choice. They too should be allowed to dress as they so wish. All you do is to turn off your face if you think their mode of dressing is offensive to you.

SAGIR: Go on.

TANI: Again, you don't patronize prostitutes, you don't visit brothels and you don't drink alcohol so what is your business with those who choose to follow those paths? If you are so concerned about those vices and want to change them, I think you should concentrate more in enlightening Muslims not to patronize those places. And I believe by laying a good example of a pious life, the people of other religions can see the hidden wisdom in your religion. To my knowledge, it is not only the Christians that patronize those places. So, why not allow your charity to begin at home?

SAGIR: Go on.

TANI: About other things you said the government or the governor of the state is doing, they could be true but I think it's good you separate the mischievous conduct and antics of politicians from the imperative of our good relations with our Christian neighbours.

SAGIR: How?

TANI: To me, politicians are simply playing games with religion, the governor inclusive. The poor Christian masses are as oppressed as the Muslim masses. As our poor find it difficult to pay rent and tuition fees for their children so also do the Christian poor. The politicians are just playing a dangerous game with religion. The Muslim and Christian masses are all victims of a very exploitative and manipulative political elite. If trouble comes, it's the poor Muslims and the poor Christians that will die.

SAGIR: (*Shouts.*) Enough of this your unislamic leftist ideological posturing. You are derailing from your duty as a Muslim to protect and defend your religion. What kind of peace and togetherness are you preaching when Muslims are being marginalized by the government that has never hidden its disdain for Muslims and Islam? How dare you tell me that we should continue to live in this sin and oppression!

TANI: So, what do you intend to do?

SAGIR: (*Stands and poses like a fighter using the stick as a weapon.*) We will protect our religion from infidels and we will fight anybody who marginalizes or fights us.

TANI: (*Tries to persuade the husband on her knees.*) My dear, we have been living with these people for centuries. We share each other's joy and sorrow. We live as neighbours in our homes and as colleagues in our working places. Our children and theirs attend the same schools. During their Christmas, they bring chickens and goats for you to slaughter for them. How can you say those people are today your enemies?

SAGIR: I think I have said enough to convince you but it appears *shetan* has denied you seeing the truth. I'm going out to do other things. Bye. (*Walks out on his wife who remains on her knees. He moves towards the flocks. Lights out.*)

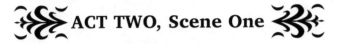

ACT TWO, Scene One

Three young graduates, STEVE, ADAM and IBRO idly sit by the roadside. They are all looking angry as they discuss their problems.

STEVE: Oh my God, today marks three years since we graduated from school yet we remain jobless, hopeless and helpless.

IBRO: This is unfortunate, our lives are just wasting.

ADAM: What kind of country is this? How can we spend all these years in school and simply end up doing nothing?

STEVE: All the promises made by the politicians since the return of democracy, they have not fulfilled them.

ADAM: To hell with this kind of democracy.

IBRO: We just have a gang of selfish and insensitive people as our leaders.

STEVE: When these politicians need our votes, they promise us all honey and milk, whenever they get to office, they simply forget us.

IBRO: Look at the governor and the local government chairman, since they won elections, they never got back to us. They changed their phone numbers and made themselves inaccessible.

ADAM: I can never forget how we laboured day and night to do all sorts of good and dirty things for them to win.

STEVE: I remember during the elections time, I didn't sleep for three days, moving to all cranies of this town and even the remotest of villages to get these people elected, but see where I am now.

IBRO: Did you know that three days before the elections, the chairman came to my house at midnight?

ADAM: Really, for what?

IBRO: He came in the company of two of his campaign aides. He wanted me to lead a gang of people to go to the house of his rival candidate, Maisango to beat him.

ADAM: Did you?

IBRO: Yes, he gave me some ten thousand naira and promised that if I finish the job, and when he eventually wins, he would give me a hundred thousand naira and a job. Since he won, I went to him over ten times. He will always defer till tomorrow. He has now even blocked me from seeing him. Each time I go, his security detail will tell me that he is busy, he is in a meeting, this and that. He has even stopped picking my phone calls. I really regret working for this man.

STEVE: For me I had a terrible experience.

IBRO: Really?

STEVE: Yes, three days before the elections, the chairman printed thousands of illegal ballot papers. I was the one who conveyed the papers to a secret warehouse in the outskirts of town. We spent the next two days massively thumb-printing the papers.

IBRO: Really?

STEVE: Not just that, I led the group that snatched ballot boxes from the election officers, in areas the chairman was losing.

ADAM: I led the operation that burnt down the campaign office of Maisanjo, but you won't believe that up till now, I'm yet to be paid.

IBRO: They used us when they needed us and dumped us when in power.

STEVE: They don't just use us but also set us up against each other. You couldn't believe that our pastor told us to vote for Joseph of Ward 8 for councillor simply because he came to the church and said he will help Christians and defend their interest when he wins, since he won nobody has heard of him.

ADAM: Indeed, I have heard of him. He is now building a magnificent palace in the outskirt of the town. He rides in an expensive car nowadays, the very boy that could barely feed himself.

IBRO: The same thing goes with Councillor Musa of Ward 9. He too came to the mosque and campaigned that he would defend Islam and Muslims when elected. We have not heard from him since then. The gate of his house now even bears a signpost "Beware of Dog". Nowadays, he is so snobbish and arrogant because he has accumulated a lot of money.

(*Enter* GAMBO.)

GAMBO: Greetings! Hello, guys, what is going on here? You sound so tense and angry.

STEVE: Yes, we are just discussing how these useless politicians have used us and dumped us in this useless democracy.

GAMBO: Come on, guys, democracy can't be said to be useless. It's the best form of government even though I concur with you that the behaviour of our political class is bad.

IBRO: If I were in your shoes, I will say the same. You have a good job now, you can't call this democracy useless, but for the rest of us it is as good as a used tissue paper.

GAMBO: It's not because I have a job but I think you should appreciate the fact that our country is now free from military dictatorship, our people are freer even though we have challenges as a country, I believe.

STEVE: What is the meaning of freedom if I don't have a job and I cannot feed properly?

GAMBO: But you can express yourself and there are boundless opportunities in a democracy you can exploit.

IBRO: The only freedom of a hungry man is food. The freedom of a jobless man is employment and not expression that will lead to nothing.

ADAM: (*Looks at* GAMBO *in surprise.*) Gambo, you look so comfortable. I'm not surprised you are defending this suffocating democracy of yours.

GAMBO: With freedom came opportunity even though there are challenges. This I want you to understand. It's not because I'm comfortable but because I remember that we were worse off under military regime.

STEVE: I don't think we were worse off under military rule. At least under the military there was security in the country. Nowadays, violence and indiscriminate killings of people are the order of the day.

IBRO: That is piffle. This is a freedom that kills.

GAMBO: I don't share your revision of history. How could you say there was security under the military when people were simply arrested and locked up in the cells for criticizing their regime?

IBRO: Under the military, people were locked up and under democracy, people are indiscriminately killed. Which one is better?

GAMBO: The violence going on is a challenge but it's also a phase. I believe that as our democracy matures, it shall fade.

STEVE: We are already fading because we are jobless. You are even adding weight and looking fresher. This system really favours people like you. I have no apologies to say that I prefer military rule.

GAMBO: (*Angrily.*) What a disgusting thing for you to say! Have you forgotten how the world hated us for being under military rule? Have you forgotten how we became a pariah state? Have you forgotten how the world imposed sanctions on our country? Have you forgotten how the military looted our treasury and sent assasins after dissenters? Have you forgotten how our prisons were filled with political prisoners? Have you forgotten how newspapers and magazines were proscribed? Have you forgotten how the labour union, the academic union, the students union were banned? Have you forgotten the draconian decrees?

IBRO: Now that we are not a pariah state and there is no sanctions, how has that benefitted the common man in our cities and the peasants in our villages?

ADAM: You called military regime corrupt, can you objectively compare the thievery under military rule with the scandalous roguery and larceny taking place now?

GAMBO: But at least now you can speak out against corruption but at that time, you couldn't.

STEVE: We thought with the restoration of democracy there would be food on the table. We thought it would bring an end to the debilitating and paralyzing poverty, hunger and want in the country. We thought freedom would mean good things of life for us. We thought the Western world that was pressuring us to restore democracy would indeed help us.

IBRO: Military rule imprisoned dissenters. Our kind of democracy imprisons the whole society.

GAMBO: How?

IBRO: Governance has become a criminal enterprise. Our politicians see public service as self-service. They have imprisoned everyone by impoverishing everyone. They steal our money and stack it in Swiss accounts.

STEVE: As no more Swiss is Dubai, Singapore, Malaysia and co.

IBRO: That's right. They sold public firms to themselves in the name of privatization. They looted and diverted money that should go to education, health and infrastructure. They buy private jets with public funds and build private estates. They buy shares for their children and wives in foreign companies.

ADAM: They create a dynasty of poverty for our people and stockpile cash for their children.

IBRO: They destroy public hospitals and build private clinics for their families. They have pauperized our people in the name of democracy.

STEVE: They interchange political positions: a governor today becomes a senator tomorrow. A senator tomorrow becomes an ambassador next. An ambassador today becomes a minister tomorrow. We are jobless, our people are disenfranchised and frustrated. This is no democracy. There cannot be peace here.

ADAM: Gambo, you are our friend but you are defending this rotten system. You are defending this inequity and injustice. You are comfortable but take my word, do not deceive yourself: on the day of trouble, a day of reckoning, you will be consumed.

GAMBO: (*Feels uncomfortable with all their attacks.*) I think you guys are too angry to reason. I have to go. Bye. (*Leaves.*)

IBRO: Go, go. We shall meet on the day of trouble and you will tell us all you know about this democracy you so much cherish.

STEVE: They think we are shiftless. A hungry man is an angry man and they will see the anger caused by the hunger they cause.

ADAM: Gambo is a dim. Just because he is living comfortably he thinks he can insult our sensibilities. Such a lickspittle.

IBRO: He is a dolt. How can any sensible human defend this blatant injustice that pervades our country?

STEVE: To me, he's a prat. Do you know I went looking for a job with the police force?

IBRO: Really?

STEVE: Yes, but I had to jettison the idea when I was given an impossible condition.

IBRO: What condition?

STEVE: (*In anger.*) I was asked to pay the sum of 100 thousand naira as bribe.

IBRO: What?

STEVE: A hundred thousand naira before I am enlisted.

IBRO: That's shocking. No wonder these policemen are corrupt. Their rot starts from the root.

ADAM: As for me, I responded to an advertisement in one of the government ministries and when I went there, I found out that it was just a charade.

IBRO: A charade?

ADAM: (*Angrily.*) Yes, they had already finished recruitment. One of the guys who was successful told me that he had to bring a letter from a big shot or else nobody would have listened to him. And I didn't even know who could give me such a letter.

IBRO: (*Angrily.*) With all these frustrations, I have no other place to vent my anger but on the government and the politicians.

STEVE: On the day of trouble I will personally lead the destruction of their properties and the burning of their houses.

ADAM: Many of them deserve to be shot.

IBRO: Much more than that.

(Lights out.)

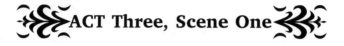 ACT Three, Scene One

An arena on campus. Lights meet three friends MAHDI, SAKA *and* YAKUBU *sitting with their school bags hung on their backs.*

SAKA: Did you guys hear that the boy Mutallab who attempted to blow up an American plane was sentenced to life in prison?

YAKUBU: Really?

SAKA: Yes, he was found guilty by the US court and sentenced.

YAKUBU: Oh, too bad. Such a boy from a privileged home has dared to ruin his life.

SAKA: I'm sure he must have caused his parents such an emotional stress and now he is in it forever.

YAKUBU: That is sad for such a young man with a bright future who decided to take the perilous and evil path of terror.

SAKA: He must have been wrongly educated or simply indoctrinated.

YAKUBU: Or brainwashed to doom.

SAKA: People often say poverty and misery lead people to the path of terror but how can anyone explain such a situation with a boy from such a wealthy home and educated in the best of schools money can buy and now choosing to kill others and ruin himself?

MAHDI: He must have been driven by the force of faith and the strength of his conviction. I see him as a spunky lad.

SAKA: Come on, Mahdi, what faith can drive such a person to decide to take the lives of others? (*They sit down at the foot of the tree, bringing out snacks and drinks from their bags to share.*)

MAHDI: Well, Islam and martyrdom.

YAKUBU: Get off it, this is not Islam. This is not martyrdom. It's simply evil.

SAKA: Islam forbids the killing of any soul unlawfully, what that boy attempted to do is not in any way Islamic and it's not martyrdom. It's sheer nonsense.

MAHDI: Well to me what he did is a jihad. A jihad against the enemies of Islam.

YAKUBU: Who are the enemies of Islam?

MAHDI: The United States and the West.

YAKUBU: And even if the US is the enemy of Islam, what role did the innocent souls in the plane he wanted to kill play?

MAHDI: The United States too has been killing innocent Muslims in other countries.

SAKA: Look, Mahdi, suicide bombing is unislamic. Any Muslim who deliberately kills himself or kills others will not enter paradise. He or she will end in hell.

YAKUBU: Even if Muslims must revenge, I don't think it's right to kill other innocent souls in the name of revenge.

SAKA: A jihad has its laid down rules in Islam; not to kill women and children, not to kill the innocent,

40

not to kill non-combatants; how do you justify such a hideous act of terror?

MAHDI: Suicide bombing is the only weapon of the weak against the strong.

YAKUBU: And it's a path to hell.

MAHDI: Why don't you people look at the atrocities and criminality perpetrated by the United States against Muslims worldwide instead of just harping on the effect.

SAKA: Mahdi, there is no justification for the killing of civilians in the name of jihad.

MAHDI: But if those civilians are Muslims, there is justification for that, right?

SAKA: I do not think the US is an enemy to Muslims or Islam.

MAHDI: (*Bursts into laughter.*) Then you must be a mad man.

SAKA: I'm not mad, I am serious. I have my points. But I will prefer you tell me your reasons for holding the belief that the US is an enemy of Islam.

MAHDI: Okay. One, for decades, America has continued to aid and abet and fund the state of Zionist Israel to occupy Palestine lands and kill innocent people in Gaza and the West Bank. America has continued to back the evil, repressive and satanic misdeeds of the state of Israel which include, killing, arresting and jailing of Palestinians. America has continued to block any attempt at the United Nations to sanction or punish Israel. Israel with the backing of the United States has for years imposed a blockage on Gaza turning the wide strip into a prison. Israel with the help of America has continued to violate all international laws. They kill and maim Muslims with impunity and with the help of American military machine and cash. Is America not an enemy of Islam?

SAKA: Number two.

MAHDI: Using the pretext of September 11 attacks, the US invaded Afghanistan and thereby killing thousands of innocent people, innocent civilians; people who had nothing to do with the attacks including people at wedding ceremonies and birthday events. They destroyed the country in the pursuit of their hegemonic agenda to dominate and rule the world.

SAKA: Three.

MAHDI: Using the pretext of search for weapons of mass destruction, the US invaded Iraq and killed thousands of people and threw the country into sectarian violence. Is America not an enemy of Islam?

SAKA: Four.

MAHDI: The United States military has continued to use drones to kill innocent civilians in western Pakistan. Hundreds of women and children have lost their lives in such daily unprovoked attacks. Is the US not an enemy of Islam?

SAKA: Five.

MAHDI: While the state of Israel has continued to keep a stockpile of nuclear weapons, America has continued to threaten and sanction Iran not for anything but because it's a Muslim country.

SAKA: Six.

MAHDI: The United States aided and funded the Mubarak regime in Egypt for decades while the regime continued to arrest, slaughter and maim innocent citizens of its country.

SAKA: Seven.

MAHDI: America aided Ethiopia to invade Somalia today.

SAKA: Eight.

MAHDI: America supported the so-called Algerian secular government to continue to suppress Muslims in that country.

SAKA: Nine.

MAHDI: The US that prides itself as a bastion of democracy and land of freedom continues to protect and support autocratic Arab monarchical dictatorships who suppress and kill their people and unleash a regime of terror.

SAKA: Ten.

MAHDI: In Yemen, hundreds of lives of civilians are lost via the use of drone attacks and backing for the tyrannical Saleh regime by the United States.

SAKA: Eleven.

MAHDI: Hundreds of Muslims are currently imprisoned in Guantanamo Bay by the United States; kept there in the most absurd and humiliating manner.

SAKA: Twelve.

MAHDI: The images of Abu Gharaib prison, the torturing of Muslims in the name of water boarding and the burning of the Qur'an by American troops in Afghanistan is another blasphemous enmity of the crude America. Now tell me of what use is America, the great *shetan,* to Muslims?

SAKA: Okay.

YAKUBU: (YAKUBU *who has been listening all the while speaks*.) Wait, Saka, before you answer, I will like to take him on all those points he raised.

MAHDI: I'm all ears.

YAKUBU: We need to understand and appreciate that no other country in the world has so much hosted and invested on peace between Israel and the Palestinians like the United States. You should not forget that from Camp David to Madrid and Oslo peace talks, the US has done a lot in terms of trying to find an end to this problem. But for the role of the US in putting restrain on Israel, it could have been worse.

MAHDI: I'm listening.

YAKUBU: American-led attack on Afghanistan is not unprovoked. We should be objective. The September 11 attacks killed over three thousand people including Muslims. And the Taliban government in Afghanistan was sheltering the terror group that perpetrated such a heinous crime. After all repeated calls for the Taliban to hand over the terrorists, they refused. American action in Afghanistan is justified because no nation will fold its arms and watch her citizens killed without any response.

MAHDI: I'm listening.

YAKUBU: I'm surprised you are citing the issue of Iraq. Saddam Hussein was not running an Islamic government. He was never a defender of Islam. He was simply a cruel and brutal dictator who killed his people at will.

MAHDI: I'm glad you are saying that. He was indeed a brutal and cruel dictator. America funded and armed to wage war against Iran for twelve years.

YAKUBU: Notwithstanding, Saddam was a monster. His ouster is justified. He was a man with a predilection for evil.

MAHDI: There are other monsters like Israel and other repressive and equally brutal monarchies America refused to overthrow. Anyway, go on, I'm listening.

YAKUBU: The use of drones to kill civilians in western Pakistan is regrettable but we need to also understand that western Pakistan is awash with home grown terrorists and runaway Al Qaeda militants from Afghanistan. Their evil ideology and violence unleashes a regime of fear and violence in those tribal areas. They live by the sword, it's okay if they die by the sword.

MAHDI: Hmm, I'm listening.

YAKUBU: About nuclear weapons, well, it is unislamic for a nation to possess such a weapon of mass murder. Because Israel owns nuclear weapons does not make it right for others.

MAHDI: So, Muslims should simply sit like ducks for Israel to launch nuclear weapons against them? Is that okay with you as a Muslim?

YAKUBU: Well, Iran has not itself admitted to having a programme of nuclear weapons for military purposes. It has always said it is for civilian use but I don't believe them. Iran is actually a serious threat to Muslim nations in the Gulf and in the Middle East. It's a state sponsor of terror which is unislamic. It is the chief backer of Hezbullah and Hamas whom are all terror groups. I do not think that Muslim countries can trust Iran with nuclear weapons. So it's not just about America or Israel but it's about Iran posing a threat to the peace and security of the region. Iran has no respect for international law. It has consistently violated UN resolutions and remained dubious about its nuclear aim.

MAHDI: Which of the UN resolutions has the state of Israel ever respected? Which international law has the state of Israel ever respected? Why has the International Atomic Agency not visited Israel? Why couldn't the UN sanction Israel? Have you forgotten what the Goldstone report said about Israeli atrocities? Why were the US and the West silent when it came to dealing with the crime of Zionism? The government of Israel is killing Palestine every day and the world is looking the other way, but when it comes to the issue of Iran, it's sanction all the way.

YAKUBU: But Israel is not a signatory to the IAEA.

MAHDI: So, because they are not signatory, it gives them the impunity to threaten and one day use it against our people? Anyway, go on, I'm listening.

YAKUBU: You really need to understand that Al Qaeda and Al Shabab are all terrorist organizations; I have no sympathy for them. They are just destroying the image of Islam. They are mass murderers. American action against them is right.

MAHDI: If you put together the number of people killed by America in Afghanistan, Iraq, Yemen and those killed by Israel in Palestine, there is no better label that defines America than being called a nation of evil and murder.

YAKUBU: That's irrational.

MAHDI: Look, my friend. America is the number one enemy of the Muslim world. America's desire is to dominate the Muslim world on behalf of the Jews. As far as the West is concerned whether you call yourself a moderate or an extremist, they see all Muslims as terrorists.

YAKUBU: You are just being sensational.

MAHDI: It's not about being sensational. It's being factual. It's only Muslims that the West called terrorists.

YAKUBU: What do you mean?

MAHDI: Hitler is not called a terrorist because he was not a Muslim. Stalin was not, Pinochet was not; all are not terrorists. Even Timothy Mcveigh, the Oklahoma bomber, James Holmes the Aurora shooter and Anders Brevik, the man who killed over seventy children in Norway, were not called terrorists because they are not Muslims. Tell me more of what use is America and the West to Muslims?

SAKA: For all I know, the American people have in many times also stood by Muslims.

MAHDI: I'm listening.

SAKA: America stood by the Muslim people of Afghanistan. It supported and funded the Mujahideen Islamic resistance that ended the Soviet occupation and the puppet government of Najibullah.

MAHDI: OK.

SAKA: The massacre and persecution of Muslims in Bosnia by Slobodan Milosevic in Yugoslavia could not have ended without the American-led military action that has today led to the independence of Bosnia and Kosovo, all Muslim nations, in Europe.

MAHDI: I'm listening.

SAKA: Without the Americans' action, Slobodan and his Serb Generals could not have been put on trial for the senseless and cruel killing of Muslims.

MAHDI: Uhum.

SAKA: America has consistently objected to and condemned the killing and maiming of Muslims in Chechnya by Russia.

MAHDI: Hmmhmm.

SAKA: American troops are currently stationed in Saudi Arabia and other Muslim Arab nations providing security against invasion or any form of attack.

MAHDI: I'm listening.

SAKA: The US has granted political asylum to thousands of Muslims from Somalia, North Africa and the Middle East who flee war, political persecution or tyranny.

MAHDI: I'm listening.

SAKA: The US has morally and financially supported the Arab Spring, to help Muslims free themselves from totalitarian rules.

MAHDI: Are you done?

SAKA: Your hatred for America is pure sentiment and unfounded. The freedom Muslims enjoy in the States is not available in most Islamic countries.

MAHDI: (*Angrily.*) You are the one that is sentimental about this issue. I think I have enough of your rankling plaudits for evil.

SAKA: Thank you.

(Lights out.)

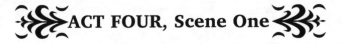

ACT FOUR, Scene One

Dim light on stage. Muslims and Christians fighting: people running helter skelter, women and children crying, fire and smoke, people carrying goods from people. Noise of clashing machetes and other weapons of war. Light comes in to reveal corpses of both Muslims and Christians, police and soldiers on patrol giving orders. Light out. Light back on stage revealing JOHN and his wife MARTHA, treating his wounds.

MARTHA: (*Crying.*) This is exactly what I have been warning you against. We have been living in peace in this town for generations, now our town totters.

JOHN: You need to understand that we have to teach these Muslims a lesson, not to dare Islamize us.

MARTHA: Now, what lesson have you taught them? Killings everywhere, human corpses litter the streets, our market burnt and shops looted and we have been locked up here in our homes like prisoners.

JOHN: But at least now they know that they don't have the monopoly of extremism or violence.

MARTHA: Christianity is about peace not violence. You went to fight them, now all of us are suffering and bearing the brunt. Our churches are burnt in your hopeless attempt to drive 'non-indegenes' and now you are claiming to teach them a lesson.

JOHN: As the only way to save our town and our children from being forced into another religion.

MARTHA: Now you are back here with wounds. Hospital is overcrowded with casualties. There is no electric power. The taps are dry. Our food reserve in the house is finished. There's no way to go out to even buy anything. Our children cannot go to school. Our people have been killed. Can you tell me realistically what we have achieved by this senseless violence?

JOHN: If we did not fight, these people could have finished us all. Did you not see the text message in circulation?

MARTHA: What text message?

JOHN: The text message that Muslims were going to attack and kill us *en masse* in our homes this Sunday?

MARTHA: So, it's because of a text message that you people chose the road of violence? Don't you know anybody, even a criminal who wants to loot can just sit down and write and circulate inciting text messages? Why didn't you people verify before you started fighting?

JOHN: But it has happened in other places. Must we wait until they raid and kill us in our homes? I'm sure if they had invaded this house and met you here, you could not have been talking by now.

MARTHA: My Bible abhors violence. For every soul you kill, you shall account for it on the day of judgment. You people are not fighting for God. You are fighting for land, vanity. What you did was ungodly.

JOHN: My conscience tells me to defend my land and my religion. How can you call yourself a Christian and you just sit down for another religion to be imposed on you. Peace? What peace? What did you read in the Bible?

MARTHA: Read Psalms 11:5; "The soul of the Lord hates those who love violence."

JOHN: Go on.

MARTHA: And Psalms 17:4; "I have kept myself from the ways of the violent."

JOHN: Three.

MARTHA: Psalms 34:14; "Turn from evil, do good; seek peace and pursue it."

JOHN: I'm listening.

MARTHA: Psalms 140:1-2; "Protect me from the violent who stir up wars continually."

JOHN: Go on.

MARTHA: Matthew 5:9; "Blessed are the peacemakers for they will be called sons of God". And Romans 14:19 says, "make every effort to do what leads to peace"; and Romans 12:21 says, "overcome evil with good". And Luke 6:17, "love your enemies; bless those who frustrate you."

JOHN: Ride on.

MARTHA: Matthew 5:43 says "love your enemies, pray for your persecutors". And Psalms 20:7 says, "some trust in chariots and some in horses, but we trust in the name of the Lord our God". Also 1 Corinthians 7:15 says, "God has called us to live in peace". And your decision to go and fight is addressed in 1 Peter 2:23 which states, "He (Jesus) did not retaliate, He made no threat". And if what you are doing is to Christianity, check 2 Corinthians 10:3 which affirms that for though we live in the world, we do not wage war as the world does.

JOHN: I'm listening.

MARTHA: Also 1 Corinthians 14:33 says, "God is not a God of disorder but of peace". And Romans 12:17 says. "Return no one evil for evil, live at peace with one another". Killing is not a way for an ideal Christian as John 18:11 says, "Jesus said Peter put your sword into your sheath". Peace is the way of our religion and should be our life. Hebrews 12:14 says, "make every effort to live in peace with all men and be holy".

JOHN: I think I have heard enough of this. One thing you must understand is that the die is cast, the battle line is drawn between us and the Muslims. Muslims are inherently violent people. Wherever they are, they seek to dominate and unleash violence; they are persecuting Christians in Egypt, in Syria, Iran, Pakistan, Malaysia and Indonesia.

MARTHA: But this is Nigeria.

JOHN: Look, Muslims have no accommodating spirit. They have no tolerance. Their idea of a society is the one ruled under Sharia law with Christians made to pay tax. Is that what you want us to succumb to?

MARTHA: Now you have led us to crisis and bloodshed. And this town will never be the same again.

(*Lights out.*)

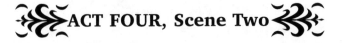# ACT FOUR, Scene Two

The home of SAGIR *and* TANI. SAGIR *has bruises on his face and also has a broken leg.* TANI *treats his wounds.*

SAGIR: (*Shouts.*) Clean the wound gently.

TANI: (*Calmly.*) My dear, this is all I have been warning you against. Of what benefit is this religious violence?

SAGIR: (*Aggressively.*) This is a holy war. It's not for worldly benefit. It is a commandment from God that Muslims should defend their religion and propagate it without hindrance.

TANI: My dear, I warned you against this Puritanism and religiosity. It's a dangerous ideology that can only unleash violence between us and the Christians.

SAGIR: I'm wondering how you seem to hold sympathy for these infidels.

TANI: It's not about sympathy, it's about the need to live in peace with our Christian neighbours.

SAGIR: What peace? How can we live in peace with the people that hate us? Look, don't you see how we bought a piece of land for our Eid prayer but the state governor acting in cohort with his Christian brothers denied us? Don't you see how soldiers and police and the intelligence agencies are arresting, killing and maiming Muslims?

TANI: Fighting Christians is not Islamic. A hand stained with blood cannot open the door of heaven.

SAGIR: Even when they are killing us?

TANI: Well, there are Hadiths and Qur'anic verses that reinforce that.

SAGIR: I'l like to hear them.

TANI: There is a Hadith that says, "The person is nearest to God who pardons, when he has someone in his power, one who would have injured him". And another hadith makes it clear that, "faith is a restraint against all violence, let no mumin commit violence".

SAGIR: I'm listening.

TANI: Another Hadith says, "God is unity and likes unity". And Qur'an 16:128 clarifies that Allah is with those who restrain themselves. Al Mumatta 47:12 says, "A strong person is not the person who throws his adversary to the ground. A strong person is the one who contains himself when he is angry". Another hadith affirms that, "all people belong to God's family and God favours best those who are most useful to God's family".

SAGIR: Are you done?

TANI: A Hadith by Bukhari reinforces that, "shedding of blood will be the matter about which judgment will be given on the day of resurrections". A similar Hadith points to the fact that, "A believer will construe to find ample scope in his religion as long as he does not kill any unlawfully".

SAGIR: Can't you for goodness sake understand that these Christians are evil? They are a bunch of sinful lots who do nothing but eat pork, eat dog, drink beer, walk naked and kill Muslims.

TANI: I don't think it's right to despise the Christians and depict them that way. They are people of the Book and our religion enjoins us to consider them as such. Didn't you read about the shelter given to Muslim refugees by the Christian king of Ethiopia, Negrus? Have you not read about how our great prophet gave protection and shelter to the Christians? Why can't you people learn from that?

SAGIR: I appreciate your thoughts and your reasoning. I appreciate your spiritual quotations. But you can't raise the flag of unity and peace when your neighbour is determined to kill you.

TANI: How can you agitate for a purist society in a heterogenous setting and accuse the other side of starting the fire? Aren't you knowledgeable as regards what happened in Lebanon in the early 80s? People like you want us to be like Iran or Saudi but it's certain we are heading to Sudan or Somalia. Religion is a free choice.

SAGIR: It's not a free choice. As Muslims we must live as Muslims and be governed by Islamic injunctions and principles.

TANI: But you can't force anyone to live by your principles if he or she does not profess your religion.

SAGIR: Christianity is a religion but Islam is more than a religion. It's a way of life. That is Sharia. These people you call Christians don't live like Christians. They live like Westerners. They endure Western liberal values, customs and vices. If they don't want to live by the teachings of their religion we want to live by the teaching of ours.

TANI: I think I prefer the freedom of the liberal societies to the religiosity of the theocracies you are talking about.

SAGIR: What do you mean?

TANI: Those Islamic theocracies are nothing but glorified tyrannies. They raise the flag of Islam only to unleash a regime of fear and torture in their land.

SAGIR: How?

TANI: (*Sternly.*) The Saudi is not a model society. The monarchy simply manipulates religion to justify their grip on power. They appropriate all the oil minerals of the state to their so-called noble family. They execute only the poor. They jail dissenters, they torture suspects in their cells; they deny women their rights even to drive; they outlaw protests; they treat black people as third-class citizens.

SAGIR: (*Angrily.*) How dare you say such a malicious thing about such a holy country?

TANI: All I said are facts: I prefer to live and worship my God in a secular country than an authoritarian theocracy of the monarch or the mullahs.

SAGIR: You have derailed. I regret spending my precious time with you. Just go.

TANI: (*She walks away.*) Now our great town will never be the same again.

(*Lights out.*)

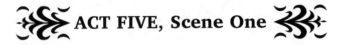

Office of the governor, a well-decorated office with five cushions. The photograph of the president is hung on the wall. The flag of the country on his table. A security council meeting is about to start. Two AIDES, *the* POLICE HEAD, *and the* ARMY CHIEF *are in attendance.*

GOVERNOR: I welcome you all.

ALL: Thank you, Your Excellency.

GOVERNOR: This emergency meeting I have called is to discuss the crisis at hand. I mean the security challenge that is threatening our peace, stability and coexistence. I'm deeply concerned about the growing disorder, lawlessness and intolerance that is degenerating to violence and vandalism. I know you are all working on it but I need to hear from you all directly on how we can end this violence.

SOLDIER: Your Excellency, we are on top of the situation. We have killed over a hundred of these troublemakers and we have arrested over a thousand of them.

POLICE: Sir, our cells are full to the brim with these criminals. We have also set up checkpoints in almost all the major roads and entrance roads to our city. We are pursuing them and will crush the remaining on the run.

GOVERNOR: Oh really!

AIDE I: Sir, I beg to differ in the way the soldiers and

58

the police are handling the prevailing security challenge.

GOVERNOR: Oh really? Why?

AIDE I: The security forces are violating the fundamental rights of our people in the guise of discharging their duties to end the violence.

GOVERNOR: Do you talk of human rights in a situation where violent elements are killing people in the name of religion?

AIDE I: We are in a democracy. And I think it's rational that we balance our security needs with our human rights obligation.

SOLDIER: What right does a man have if he picks up a gun to snuff the life of another man?

POLICE: We are talking of peace and security and you are talking of rights. So, in the name of human rights we should fold our arms and watch people kill people? That is preposterous.

AIDE I: Restoring law and order is not a blank cheque to kill, arrest, humiliate and detain.

GOVERNOR: Wait, wait, wait, what exactly do you mean?

AIDE I: The soldiers and the police are killing more innocent persons than getting at the violent ones. They kill indiscriminately. They cordon off places, violate privacies and raid homes, offices and schools.

POLICE: What do you expect us to do when people give cover to these criminals? That is a scurrilous statement. We do our job in the most sedulous ways.

AIDE I: I believe you are trained to do your job as professionals. This is an elected government, you can't continue to harass and intimidate people who voted us into office in the name of going after violent people.

GOVERNOR: Come on! These people are doing their job. Don't you see the danger and the dire state of things? Our security men and women are human beings, too. They have families. Don't you see how they put their lives in danger?

AIDE I: Your Excellency, they carry no mandate and are not accountable but we are.

GOVERNOR: I know, but the US, the bastion of democracy, themselves have to shove aside human rights to fight terror, don't you hear of the Patriots Act?

AIDE I: The level of arbitrariness and cruelty of our security enforcement agents is uncomparable, Sir.

GOVERNOR: Come on! Don't tell me that New York, Los Angeles, London, Paris and Rome police give ice cream to rioters. Look, I have a constitutional duty to protect the lives and property of the citizens.

AIDE I: And the citizens have the constitutional rights to be protected from abuse, Sir.

GOVERNOR: (*Turns.*) You people, what are your major challenges? And what do you need to make it easier for you to discharge your duties?

POLICE: Sir, our major problems are shortage of money, shortage of equipment and the unwillingness of the public to bring information of the hideouts of these criminals.

GOVERNOR: (*Turns to* AIDE I.) And what do you advise on this?

AIDE I: Your Excellency, the public are unwilling to give out information not without a reason.

GOVERNOR: And what is the reason?

AIDE I: The police betray informants by revealing their identity to the killers for a fee.

POLICE: How dare you say that? That's a wild allegation.

AIDE I: Five boys were three days ago slaughtered a day after they gave information to the police on the hideouts of some terrorists.

POLICE: And what are your proofs that we revealed their identity?

AIDE I: They could not have betrayed themselves. And you did not do anything to protect them.

GOVERNOR: So, what are you doing about this?

POLICE: Sir, we are intensifying the search for these killers.

AIDE I: The police have never found the killers of anybody. I don't believe they will this time. And about their request for more money and equipment, I have a word to add.

GOVERNOR: Go ahead.

AIDE I: Extra budgetary money allocated to the police never goes to the rank and file. It stops with the officers and that is why the lower ranks work with frustration and extort money from the general public.

(*Enter* COMMISSIONER. *The* AIDES *salute at his entrance.*)

GOVERNOR: Why did you gatecrash into this meeting and why are you sweating and looking so dishevelled?

COMMISSIONER: Sir, it's an emergency.

GOVERNOR: What is it?

COMMISSIONER: (*Stammering.*) Just some few minutes ago, there was a bomb explosion near the central cinema.

POLICE: What, bomb explosion?

COMMISSIONER: Yes, bomb explosion. It shuddered the city.

GOVERNOR: Oh my God, anyone killed?

COMMISSIONER: Yes, about ten people were killed and thrice that injured.

GOVERNOR: This is dastardly. We have to rush there. You have to apprehend these criminals.

SOLDIER: We will, Sir. It is our duty. We will cordon off the area and punish all those who live around the area of the blast.

AIDE I: That is extreme and unethical. This is exactly what I'm saying; you just want to punish innocent people. A bomb explodes and you punish people around the neighbourhood. That is wild.

SOLDIER: You are just a politician. You know nothing about security. There is no other way to discourage people from harbouring terrorists and criminals than this. If we are to go by your human rights sermon, the whole of this country will be annihilated by violent thugs.

GOVERNOR: Let us not argue and fight over this. It has happened already. Brigadier, we all know it is your duty to ensure our security. I will advise that you work hand in hand with other security personnel to bring the perpetrators to book. Meanwhile, deploy your boys to the scene. I want to visit the place.

(*They all rush out of the office as the* GOVERNOR *steps out. Lights out.*)

ACT FIVE, Scene Two

The meeting continues as they return from the scene of the bomb blast.

GOVERNOR: These terrorists have no conscience. How can you explode a bomb in such a place? What kind of cause are they pursuing? This is ungodly and inhuman. No faith condones murder.

POLICE: These people are not religionists, they are just murderers.

AIDE II: Your Excellency, I suggest the need to reach out to them. To hear their grievances on why they do all these.

POLICE: I don't think it's necessary.

SOLDIER: They should just be crushed. We will continue to seek them, find them and flush them.

GOVERNOR: Why do you say we should reach out to them after they have killed and committed such act of genocide?

AIDE I: Well, Your Excellency, some months ago, I wrote a portentous memo to you. I drew your attention to the fact that the attitude of our security agents can lead to a lot of consequences. The police raided a mosque in the east suburb and shot at the Imam. An Imam that has over five thousand students. Logically such people can't just fold their arms and watch.

GOVERNOR: You are right. But what has that got to do with blasting a bomb in a crowded place?

POLICE: Well, Your Excellency, we are law enforcement agents. We won't tolerate anyone hiding behind religion to incite the public. We entered the mosque because we got hint that the cleric was hiding weapons inside. And everyone knows that cleric as a troublemaker.

SOLDIER: I have listened to his preaching. He said he does not recognize the authority of the government. He does not recognize the constitution of our country. And he openly called on his followers to kill government officials and security personnel.

POLICE: And we found three guns in his possession.

AIDE I: But those were the kinds of gun allocated to the police. There were strong suspicions that you planted them to implicate, arrest and jail him for gun running.

(*The* POLICE HEAD's *phone rings. He looks at it.*)

POLICE: Excuse me, Your Excellency. It is an emergency alert. (*He receives the call.*) A suicide bomber just crashed into a church killing many worshippers! (*The* GOVERNOR *stands. Everyone present stands too. He paces up and down.*) Listen, deploy the special squad immediately to the scene. Let the rescue team and ambulances report at the scene with immediate effect.

GOVERNOR: Oh my God. Again? This is pure evil. Any idea who they are?

COMMISSIONER: They call themselves Council for Holy War.

GOVERNOR: Holy what?

COMMISSIONER: They even issued out a statement after the blast stating their reasons.

GOVERNOR: And what are their reasons?

COMMISSIONER: They said they are avenging the killing of their members by the police. And they said they are also avenging the killing of Muslims and the burning of the mosque in the west suburbs. They accused the government of not doing anything despite their initial protestations.

GOVERNOR: That's untenable and illogical. What they are doing is not a holy war but a satanic war against innocent persons. I can't tolerate this unbridled lust for bloodshed.

COMMISSIONER: They called the suicide bomber a martyr.

POLICE: How do we handle this?

AIDE II: We need to encourage Muslim clerics to come out and condemn the killings and call for peace. We also need to reach out to the Christians not to over-react and consider this violence as an act by a violent, deranged few. This will stem revenge.

POLICE: We need to deploy bomb detectors around worship centres. All worshippers entering churches and mosques must be frisked. We should also ban the parking of cars inside the premises of the church. And there is the need to increase more checkpoints.

AIDE II: But the bombers must have passed through your checkpoints.

(*Enter* AMBASSADOR *and* MR EHUD.)

AMBASSADOR: Good afternoon, Your Excellency.

GOVERNOR: Good afternoon, Mr Ambassador. It is good that you are here. I was about going out to the scene of the bomb blast. Nevertheless, we can still talk before we go there. Have your seat.

(AMBASSADOR *sits*.)

AMBASSADOR: The government of my country is deeply concerned. And I'm asked by my President to convey to you our moral and political support towards ending the ongoing violence and the restoration of law and order.

GOVERNOR: Thank you.

AMBASSADOR: I wish to also introduce to you Mr Ehud. He is a security and defence contractor and can help with his knowledge, skill and expertise in tackling the problem of violence and terrorism.

GOVERNOR: Oh, that is good. You are welcome. (*Shakes hands and smiles*.)

EHUD: Thank you.

GOVERNOR: Is he here as part of your contribution to help us out of this problem?

AMBASSADOR: Yes and no. He is a contractor. A security contractor. Mr Ehud, you may wish to speak.

EHUD: Thank you. I'm Mr Ehud Gilaz, the CEO of Ehud Consult, an Israeli security contracting firm. We specialize in supplying and installing security surveillance equipment. We supply security gadgets such as bomb detectors, bullet-proof vests, security cameras and telephone interceptors.

GOVERNOR: Oh, that is interesting and relevant at this time. But, Mr Ambassador, I thought your country will be of help to us at this time of need but you are rather bringing a contractor.

AMBASSADOR: Yes, we will but not now.

GOVERNOR: I overheard you issuing out warning to your nationals not to come to this country because of the 'grievous security situation'.

AMBASSADOR: Yes, it is routine that we warn our countrymen to stay away from trouble spots.

GOVERNOR: But your contractors can come?

AMBASSADOR: (*Silent.*)

GOVERNOR: Well, Mr Ambassador, I have to suspend this meeting for now. I have to be at the scene of the bomb blast. I'll get in touch with you sometime this week.

AMBASSADOR: It's okay. We express our sincere sympathy on what happened. Have a great day.

GOVERNOR: Thank you.

(Lights out.)

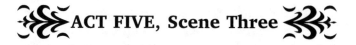

ACT FIVE, Scene Three

The GOVERNOR's *office. Back from the scene of the church bombing, the* GOVERNOR *sits with the* COMMISSIONER *and two* AIDES.

GOVERNOR: It is unimaginable that a human being with five senses can decide to blow himself up, waste his life and bring so much grief to our families in a hopeless and misinformed pursuit of a weird dream.

COMMISSIONER: They kill women and children and they call their act holy war. That is absurd. That is turpitude.

GOVERNOR: What is your view on the causes or the long-term solution to this problem?

AIDE I: Before that, Your Excellency, I have my concern on the manner this issue is being handled.

GOVERNOR: What are your concerns?

AIDE I: Your Excellency, millions of taxpayers' money is pumped into security and other areas are neglected.

GOVERNOR: What can ever function without security?

AIDE I: Your Excellency, for the past eleven months, funds meant for education, health, housing, social welfare and infrastructural development are diverted to security. I think we are just solving one problem and creating many.

GOVERNOR: If we don't restore peace, no child will go to school. If we don't restore peace, no one will invest here. If we don't restore peace, no one will live here. If we don't restore peace, no infrastructure will be meaningful. We must guarantee and safeguard the sanctity of life before we talk of anything. Monies spent on security are well spent.

AIDE I: But, Sir, they are not yielding the desired result. Security chiefs and security contractors are those benefitting. And the violence continues. As long as we will divert monies for human development, we will simply aggravate the problem. Social issues I believe are contributing factors to this crisis.

GOVERNOR: Expantiate.

AIDE I: Sir, the truth is that there is so much poverty in the land. The gap between the rich and the poor keeps expanding. Most of our elected officials have moved far away from their people. I see the factor of social injustice and exclusion in the ongoing violence.

COMMISSIONER: But the terrorists are killing poor people. And the sectarian violence is only taking place in poor neighbourhoods.

GOVERNOR: Poverty is not an excuse for violence. And these criminals perpetrating this crime did not say they are fighting poverty. They are making the claim of acting on behalf of their faith which is false because no faith advocates violence.

AIDE I: But there is no doubt that most of their foot soldiers are from poor families. I do not think it is possible for any child to agree to be a suicide bomber if our society gives him good education, employment and guarantees him some form of social security.

70

COMMISSIONER: I beg to disagree. These so-called holy warriors snatch cars, rob people and kill aimlessly and randomly. It is not poverty that drives them to kill but passion to create fear and unleash violence. I suggest we should regulate preaching, close down the religious schools that are without registrations.

GOVERNOR: That will be another trouble. It's too sensitive.

COMMISSIONER: Because religion is regarded sensitive, it gives birth to impunity.

AIDE: I think Your Excellency should unfold a social agenda to tackle poverty and end neglect which will automatically contain extremism and intolerance.

(*Enter* MESSENGER.)

MESSENGER: Good evening, Sir.

GOVERNOR: Good evening. I can't remember I sent you on an errand. Or do I have any message?

MESSENGER: Sir, it's a serious problem just now.

GOVERNOR: And what is it again?

MESSENGER: (*Dramatically sobbing.*) Yesterday night, some Christian youths raided Kuru Janta, the village at the outskirts killing over 300 Muslim women, men and children. They razed their houses and burnt their market stores. And just now some Muslim herdsmen encircled the Dogo Na Hauwa village and killed hundreds of men, women and children. They burnt down churches, houses and market stores. The two villages are now empty as most of the survivors are now spread in camps in military and police barracks.

GOVERNOR: (*Troubled.*) This is terrible. Upon all we spent on security! (*Lights out.*)

71

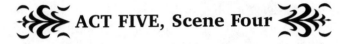# ACT FIVE, Scene Four

Evening. The GOVERNOR, *the* COMMISSIONER, *and* AIDE I & II *meet in his office. The* GOVERNOR *is in a confused state.*

GOVERNOR: (*Trembles.*) Our democracy is threatened. Our peace is threatened. This mayhem must stop. We must end this Muslim-Christian violence. I cannot condole or tolerate this. What is wrong and how can we end this? I want to hear from you.

AIDE II: Your Excellency, things have not been going right. If I am protected, I can say the bitter truth.

GOVERNOR: Why not? We are in a state of emergency. You better speak up.

AIDE II: Your Excellency, the violence between Muslim and Christians keep lingering for a number of reasons. First is the very fact that successive governments including yours have set up many probe panels the reports of which have never been implemented.

GOVERNOR: Go on.

AIDE II: Many times high profile politicians, religious leaders and traditional rulers have been implicated and indicted but you have consistently shied away from prosecuting them. And this gives ground for impunity.

GOVERNOR: Aah, me? OK, go on.

AIDE II: The organizational leadership of the Christian

and Muslim groups have consistently frustrated any attempt at prosecuting culprits by sensationalizing the cases, claiming that their members were targeted for victimization

GOVERNOR: Go on.

AIDE II: The police and the soldiers have never acted as neutrals enforcing the law. Many of them take sides with the people of their faith.

GOVERNOR: Go on.

AIDE II: Mosques and churches have become arenas for spreading hate and violence instead of love and good neighbourliness. The use of information technology through texts and social media to spread rumour and incite people is now the order of the day.

GOVERNOR: Go on.

AIDE II: The proliferation of weapons is a serious obstacle to peace. We can't end violence without blocking the source and entry of weapons in our society.

GOVERNOR: First, I cannot just order the arrest of emirs or chiefs because panels of inquiry have indicted them. You need to understand the sensitivity of this and the political repercussion of such an action. If I do that, not many people will look at the case from its substrate but I will personally be targeted. And our people will misinterpret such an action.

AIDE II: Then as long as we continue to shield those big fishes even when it is glaring that they are accomplices, peace and solution will continue to elude us.

GOVERNOR: Well, there is always a better way of getting them along. You have always reminded me that we are politicians.

AIDE II: Getting them along is not getting the problem over.

GOVERNOR: Don't forget and don't ignore their political value. They helped us win elections and we have an opposition that is ready to cash in on any crisis, I can't risk arresting any emir or chief for whatever reasons. Just keep this in mind.

AIDE I & II: Yes, Sir.

GOVERNOR: As for religious leaders, I'm quite aware of the role they are playing. But also I can't arrest and prosecute them for similar reasons.

AIDE: But a report clearly indicted church leaders of distributing weapons to their members and same thing with some Imams; should such persons continue to walk free?

GOVERNOR: If I order the arrest of those reverends and pastors and Imams, the entire Muslim and Christian population will stand up against me and my government and then we lose elections. Is that what you want? I can't do that.

AIDE I & II: Yes, Sir.

GOVERNOR: I understand the indigene/settler dichotomy is a contributory factor. But you know there are indigenes and there are indeed settlers. And the settlers have always voted for the opposition parties.

AIDE I: But the settlers pay taxes and they have been here for over three generations. And they have the constitutional right to vote for a candidate of their choice, Sir.

GOVERNOR: Yes, they do. But we must maintain a balance here not to upset our loyal voters.

AIDE I: You are right, Sir.

GOVERNOR: As for the behaviour of security agencies, I have my limitations. What we have is a federal police and a federal army. I don't have the constitutional authority to set up a police force. My hands are tied. That's why I have been agitating for a state police but the federal government is saying no.

COMMISSIONER: Well, Sir, in that aspect, I think there should be caution because if there is a state police, your successor will use it against you.

GOVERNOR: Your points are valid. But he can also use the federal police against me. And again, I cannot call for the redeployment of the commissioner of police and the army brigade commander because they really helped us during the last elections and we need them for the next one.

(*Enter* MESSENGER.)

GOVERNOR: (*Angry.*) Please I have told you I don't want to see anybody for now.

MESSENGER: Aah, Sir, there is a problem. An emergency, Sir.

GOVERNOR: And what is it this time?

MESSENGER: Gunmen on motorbike shot the chairman of your party. They also shot the head of the vigilante group.

GOVERNOR: (*Confused.*) Oh my God. This is getting out of hand. Please, inform the security chiefs about this at once.

(*Lights out.*)

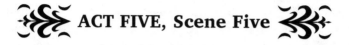

ACT FIVE, Scene Five

GOVERNOR'*s office. The* GOVERNOR *and two of his aides meeting with the* IMAM *and* PASTOR.

IMAM: Your Excellency, the dusk to dawn curfew you imposed is punitive. It has made it impossible for my people to attend to their five daily obligatory prayers. I am here to convey to you the opposition of the Muslim ummah to this curfew. God has ordered us to pray five times a day, and in congregation. But your curfew is denying us our obligation to our creator.

PASTOR: Your Excellency, the curfew you imposed has virtually made it impossible for our brethren to attend mass in the evenings and on Sundays. This curfew is denying us the right to worship our God. The house of God must be open and remain open. Our people are suffering. You cannot punish the innocent because of the guilty. We Christians are peace loving people and must not be denied our right to worship our God.

IMAM: Your Excellency, according to you, this curfew was imposed to forestall this violence. But people do not believe so.

GOVERNOR: And what do people insinuate?

IMAM: You imposed this curfew because the chairman of your party was killed. When hundreds of innocent lives were lost, you never thought of curfew. Your curfew is also impoverishing our people. Most people are poor. They have to go out of their homes to fend for their families. Markets are closed, no food; the Water Board have switched off the tap, and there is no electric power. The innocent must not suffer.

PASTOR: Since the imposition of your curfew, police and soldiers have been harassing and intimidating people. They enter into houses and arrest our children and take them away to detention.

IMAM: Right now, we have over a hundred of our children in detention in army and police cells. We demand their unconditional release in the interest of peace. And tell your policemen and soldiers that Islam forbids non-Muslims from entering mosques. They should stop in their best interest. They should also stop crashing into our homes in the name of pursuing terrorists. We are not terrorists.

PASTOR: Only yesterday, a pregnant woman was beaten by a soldier who accused her of violating the curfew simply because she was going to the hospital.

IMAM: The police shot a man who was calling for prayer at dawn. If you don't lift this curfew the blood of the innocent is on your hand.

AIDE I: Your lordships, His Excellency has heard all your complaints. We just need your understanding. This curfew is not going to be there forever. It's a temporary measure to end the violence. You as religious leaders have a role to play; talk to your people to end violence and vengeance. We cannot continue to live like this. Other nations of the world have moved on. We can't continue to kill each other.

People must respect each other's belief. The image of our country is in tatters. No one wants to come and invest in our state again. This was not how we used to live. No God and no religion advocates or propagates violence. We cannot be like Beirut of the 80s. Look at what war has done to the Sudan and Somalia. Bombings, assassinations, killings and clashes will lead us nowhere. Enough blood has been shed. The future of our country and our state and our lives is at stake. Violence does no good to anyone. Talk to your followers, they believe in you. We thank you for your visit and plead with you to cooperate with the government to find a lasting solution to this problem.

IMAM: Well, before we end this meeting, I'll like to make an observation. The tone of your speech is like we are the ones aiding, abetting or instigating people to breach the peace.

AIDE I: Not at all.

IMAM: (*Calmly*.) Hold on. It's you in government that have more to do, not us. There is so much corruption in the system. The rich are empowered and the poor are improverished the more. You must stop the purloining of public funds and use public resources for public good. Our children have no good education, no job after school, and no hope. You send your children to expensive schools, home and abroad. You build mansions and our people are homeless. You feed your dogs with canned food and our children starve to bed. You protect your families and leave us at the mercy of drunken and pernicious policemen and soldiers. When your own dies, you declare a state of emergency but when our own dies, it's business as usual. You cannot have peace if you do not have justice.

PASTOR: (*Calmly.*) What our society is facing today is not the failure of religious leaders but that of government and politicians. The Lord says you reap what you sow. You politicians have sown iniquity and evil and today we are reaping violence. The child that is uneducated and hungry is himself a weapon. We the religious leaders are doing our best but food is the god of the hungry.

(*Lights out.*)

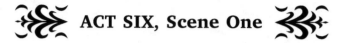 **ACT SIX, Scene One**

At the interrogation room. SHEIKH JABBAR *is at the centre of a semi-circle with three panelists ready to interrogate him. He answers all questions with arrogance.*

PANELIST 1: Sheikh Jabbar, why do you preach hate and incite people?

SHEIKH JABBAR: I don't preach hate and I don't incite people. I just preach the word of God, the Almighty, our Creator, the Creator of the heavens and the earth, the Beneficent, the Merciful.

PANELIST 2: You said you don't preach hate and you don't incite people but we have it on record where you called on your followers to stand up and fight infidels and fight the government. Who are the infidels and why should you incite your followers to subvert a constitutionally elected government?

SHEIKH JABBAR: There is no constitution except the Qur'an and there is no government except that of Allah. An infidel is a non-believer in Islam and anyone who is against Islam, and any government not established and run according to the dictates of Islam is a government of infidels.

PANELIST 2: Do you know the implication of what you are saying and what you have done?

SHEIKH JABBAR: In doing Allah's work and fulfilling his commandment, there is no implication. All you can do is to either imprison or kill me and I'm prepared for that.

PANELIST 2: The society will be better off without you and your extremist ideas.

SHEIKH JABBAR: I will be fulfilled and feel accomplished.

PANELIST 3: Why do you want to subvert our secular society?

SHEIKH JABBAR: There is no secular society in the world.

PANELIST 3: We are a democratic and secular society.

SHEIKH JABBAR: Even the United Kingdom is not a secular society, the Queen of England is the Head of the Church of England and the Archbishop of Canterbury has a seat in the House of Lords. In America you cannot be a president if you are not a Christian and uphold Christian values.

PANELIST 3: But we are a multireligious society, your theocratic advocacy can only generate crisis and violence.

SHEIKH JABBAR: No human law is above God's law. Our mission in the world is to do and live the wish of God. Those opposed to God's law are those generating crisis and violence.

PANELIST 1: Your ideas are anti-diluvian and antithetical to the tenets of democracy.

SHEIKH JABBAR: Allah's words are never archaic. Western democracy which you people are making is evil. It is a breeding ground for sin and pestilence.

PANELIST 1: How can freedom, human rights, the universal values now embraced by humanity, be called sin?

SHEIKH JABBAR: Freedom and human rights for gays, lesbians and alcoholics is not the kind of freedom I will like to be associated with.

PANELIST 2: You don't believe in freedom of human rights?

SHEIKH JABBAR: Human beings do not have freedom and rights than to obey and do the wish of the Lord, their creator.

PANELIST 1: But free nations have flourished and prospered and fared better than theocratic ones.

SHEIKH JABBAR: They flourish and prosper in sin and their crash is imminent as you can see from their economic woes. The path of the Lord is the only path of freedom.

PANELIST 2: Why do you call for the execution of Mr Gideon?

SHEIKH JABBAR: Because he blasphemed. And the punishment for blasphemy is execution.

PANELIST 2: This is a country that respects freedom of speech.

SHEIKH JABBAR: If your venal democracy respects freedom of speech, you would not have arrested me for preaching. In the Western world, Islamic preachers have been arrested and consistently facing persecution and their constitution is said to guarantee freedom of speech.

PANELIST 2: Democracy guarantees individuals the right to express all opinions.

SHEIKH JABBAR: It's a mockery. Most countries in the

Western world jail people for denying the holocaust or for anti-semitism, but condole insult against Islam as right. If Gideon has the right to insult my religion, I have the right to react.

PANELIST 2: But not to the point of killing or murder.

SHEIKH JABBAR: You cannot spit on the face of a man and dictate to him on how to react.

PANELIST 2: Who are you to judge? Who are you to fight for God? Why not leave the blasphemer to God?

SHEIKH JABBAR: If a blasphemer blasphemes alone in his room, his God will deal with him, if he does it to my ear, he has insulted my beliefs.

PANELIST 2: The state guarantees citizens their fundamental rights of speech and why not if you feel offended take the offender to court?

SHEIKH JABBAR: The state that protects a blasphemer should also educate him or her of its consequences.

PANELIST 1: If you or any of your followers insult another person's beliefs and he or she passes a sentence on you, will you be happy?

SHEIKH JABBAR: I do not insult other people's religion. I'm a man opposed to profanity.

PANELIST 1: I have listened to your tapes. You do insult people that profess other religions. You call them infidels.

SHEIKH JABBAR: They are infidels if they don't embrace Islam. Calling them infidels is no blasphemy.

PANELIST 3: Why did you call on your followers to vandalize hotels?

SHEIKH JABBAR: Hotels harbour alcohol and alcoholics

and prostitutes. They are immoral places. I did order them to tear them down.

PANELIST 3: You have no right to do so. You are being irrational. Your order has led to the killing of innocent persons who simply went to lodge. You called on people to attack the police and other security agents.

SHEIKH JABBAR: The police and other security agents represent the repressive arm of our sinful oppressive state. They are a corrupt and cruel arm of the state. The police is the only job in the world a person can do without conscience. You are just interested about what I said about the police, but you did not take cognizance of what the police are doing to us. They kept raiding our homes, our schools, intimidating us and arresting us at will. They have made life unbearable for anyone who dares to speak the truth. They molest and abuse people. They engage in extrajudicial murder. They want to deny us the right to worship our God. I, indeed, called on people to defend themselves against the police and any uniformed personnel who tries to obstruct them from performing their religious obligation.

PANELIST 3: Do you know the implication of your action? It is felony and treason to call for an attack against the police.

SHEIKH JABBAR: And it's not felony or treason for the police to kill us in our homes? You see, as long as you continue to give the police the free hand to intimidate and abuse people, peace will elude you all. They set up people on thrumped-up allegations.

They detain people at will. They shoot people at will. They make life unbearable for people. All I did was to tell people to protect themselves from the masters called the police.

PANELIST 1: You condemned science and called on parents to withdraw their children from science schools. Is it not a contradiction to be antagonistic to science and technology while you use a car, a microphone and even use cassettes and CDs and DVDs to propagate your hate speech? I can even see you wearing a wristwatch.

SHEIKH JABBAR: Knowledge of good comes from God and knowledge of evil comes from Satan. The science that I'm opposed to, and it's being taught to children in school, is mostly the science of evil. It is contrary to not only the teachings of Islam, but even I believe that of other religions.

PANELIST 2: What do you mean by that?

SHEIKH JABBAR: For example, the theory of human evolution as founded by the English scientist, Charles Darwin, is evil. Humans did not evolve. They were created by Allah. We did not evolve from apes. Humans like all animals are distinctively created. The teaching of this kind of science is incompatible with the teaching of my religion. It is an opposition to God. This kind of science is sinful. If you don't believe that God is the creator of all beings and all things then you do not believe in God. I strongly told parents not to allow their children to be misinformed by this kind of false and misleading scientific theory. Secondly, I said that the so-called

Big Bang theory as propagated by science that according to scientists led to the formation of the earth, is nothing but a blatant lie and sin. The earth was not formed by coincidence or accident. It was a wish of God. It was created by God for a purpose. The universe and all that it contains are God's creation. By the word and command of God, the universe was formed and not by the billions of years of Big Bang.

PANELIST 2: You don't like secular school and education. You call on parents to withdraw their children from school?

SHEIKH JABBAR: I did not but I don't care if my enemies misinterpret me and put words into my mouth. What I said is clear; any educational system or form of learning that undermines the values, culture and ethos of our religion must be discarded.

PANELIST 2: How can you subvert the prescriptions of your religion that encourage people to seek for knowledge and you are an obscurant?

SHEIKH JABBAR: The system of education used in these so-called secular schools is evil. It is corrupting and destructive. It has destroyed the moral values of our society and the future of our children. It has destroyed the spirit and thoughts of our kids. Our children used to respect their parents, now they don't. Our children used to take their religion seriously, now they don't. The educational system of this country now only diverts the attention of our children to entertainment and pornography. It only teaches them to sing, dance and be rude. It is a menace.

PANELIST 1: You are a vendor of illiteracy and ignorance. You cash on it to propagate bigotry and intolerance.

SHEIKH JABBAR: I'm a man opposed to any secular education that inculcates disobedience to God's laws and the ethos of my religion.

PANELIST 1: You traduce and hate the Jews and the state of Israel. We have it on record. You implore your audience to attack and kill the Jews. Your religion preaches peace and you are preaching hate and violence to exterminate the existence of others.

SHEIKH JABBAR: I did trenchantly condemn Zionism. I never recommend the killing of the Jews. The state of Israel under its Zionist rulers is a cancer to humanity and a threat to world peace. Israeli rulers oppress Muslims in Palestine by occupying their lands and denying them the right to life and living. Israeli rulers are the Hitlers of today. Israel is the real terror state. There is nowhere in the world where human beings could be so cruelly treated as in the land of Palestine. The rulers of Israel have no respect for the laws of God and even of man. They disobey international laws with impunity. They lay siege on Gaza for years and kill as much as they want and at any time they want because America is backing them. I have no apology calling on all my listeners to kill that cancer.

PANELIST 3: You sanction attacks on churches. What an evil thing to do by a man of God!

SHEIKH JABBAR: It is equally evil to attack the mosque. When a church is burnt or attacked it is a major news but when a mosque is attacked it is not news. On many occasions, Muslims have been raided and attacked and mosques set ablaze but the government and the media ignored it. If violence and vandalism is not committed by a Muslim then it is not violence and vandalism. Extremists and terrorists must be Muslims to be considered so. Whosoever does not want a church to be burnt must be up and against the burning of our mosque.

PANELIST 3: Now you want non-believers to join your religion.

SHEIKH JABBAR: Yes, I do.

PANELIST 3: How do you encourage and inspire the people you call infidels and unbelievers to join your religion if you sanction their killing and the burning of their worship centres?

SHEIKH JABBAR: No one who genuinely wants to join my religion will have to first attack me or my people or my mosque. My religion is of peace. It recommends good neighbourliness with non-believers but no surrender to evil, mischief and violence by non-believers.

PANELIST 2: Do you believe in the authority of the government and the constitution of this country?

SHEIKH JABBAR: Any government not founded on the virtuous teachings of my religion, its principles and tenets are satanic. I do not recognize and will never respect any constitution other than the one prescribed for me by my religion.

PANELIST 2: (*Angrily*.) Take him out.

(Lights out.)

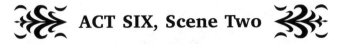

ACT SIX, Scene Two

At the interrogation room. PASTOR GATARI *is at the centre of a semi-circle facing three panelists. He is being interrogated. He is arrogant and unremorseful throughout the session.*

PANELIST 1: What is your full name?

PASTOR GATARI: I'm Pastor Gatari Ishaya.

PANELIST 1: What do you do?

PASTOR GATARI: I'm a cleric; a pastor.

PANELIST 1: You used your pulpit to virulently incite your church members to attack non-Christians?

PASTOR GATARI: I did not. I only tell them to resist any attempt by anyone or group of persons who wants to use force to take over their land or Islamize them.

PANELIST 1: You called non-Christians in your vain-glorious sermons as settlers who should either be forced out of this town or be killed. How can a man of God say so?

PASTOR GATARI: This is our land, we belong here. A bunch of strangers who came from somewhere else cannot come to force us to abandon our religion and ways of life and become them.

PANELIST 2: How do you call people settlers when they have been here for over three hundred years?

PASTOR GATARI: No matter how long a stranger stays,

a stranger is a stranger.

PANELIST 2: But it is an historical record that the people you call indigenes too came from somewhere.

PASTOR GATARI: Yes, but when they came the land was unoccupied.

PANELIST 2: Meeting an unoccupied land also does not make it your own.

PASTOR GATARI: Then whose own is it? Ghosts or what?

PANELIST 3: I thought as a preacher, a pastor and a man of God you also believe that the earth and what it contains belongs to God. And that everyone will use it and leave it here.

PASTOR GATARI: Yes, I do, but that does not mean my people should sit down and fold their arms and see some strangers take it over.

PANELIST 3: Are you a man of God who preaches the word of God or simply a fighter for land rights; land, a worldly thing that you can call vanity?

PASTOR GATARI: Protecting and defending your land is as good as defending your beliefs. One must live in a space, in a land to be able to worship his God.

PANELIST 3: And expelling non-indigenes or inciting people against them is part of your worship.

PASTOR GATARI: We did not expel them. It's the non-Christians that want to expel us the indigenes.

PANELIST 2: How?

PASTOR GATARI: They vandalize our cemetery by insisting they will not allow their deceased to be buried near Christians. They are disallowing the slaughtering of pigs in the hatchery. They said wine, spirits and alcohol must not be sold in the market. They came out at night and attacked hotels. Some of their youths even molested our women that they must cover their faces up. They want us to be like them. Live like them by force.

PANELIST 2: Do you recommend alcohol to your church members and do you encourage them to visit hotels?

PASTOR GATARI: No, I don't.

PANELIST 2: So, why are you defending alcoholics and hotel goers?

PASTOR GATARI: I'm not, but I also do not believe alcoholics should be attacked or killed and I will not support the burning of hotels by extremists and terrorists.

PANELIST 1: Who do you consider as extremists and terrorists?

PASTOR GATARI: People who are intolerant of Christians are extremists and people who believe in the use of violence and force to kill and maim Christians are terrorists.

PANELIST 1: What do you call members of your church who obeyed your incitement and raided and killed other persons that are not Christians?

PASTOR GATARI: My religion does not encourage or recommend violence. No member of my church is an extremist or terrorist. My church members will not simply agree to be subjected by a band of people who think they have the monopoly of violence and are waging a holy war against us.

PANELIST 3: You recommend vengeance. You don't believe in turning the cheek?

PASTOR GATARI: I know where you are getting at. But what you need to know is that my people and I will never ever, and I repeat: never ever submit to any attempt to exterminate our existence. We will never live under any world apart from that of Christ our lord and personal saviour.

PANELIST 1: We have it on record how some of your church members burnt mosques and attacked Muslims. Is it all part of the resistance?

PASTOR GATARI: They built their mosque on a disputed land.

PANELIST 1: Should dispute not be better resolved in a court of law than by arson as your vicious thoughts suggest?

PASTOR GATARI: Why are you not interested in the very fact that the Muslims are waging war against us and want to Islamize us? How can one come to live in my land and dictate my life and you want to say I'm wrong for saying no?

PANELIST 2: You collect tithe and donations from your church members?

PASTOR GATARI: Yes, I do.

PANELIST 2: You are a Sybarite. You have a big house, big cars and your children study in expensive schools in the Western world and here you are encouraging the children of others to kill and be killed.

PASTOR GATARI: That is the most despicable thing to say. This is my land and I'm from here. And as far as donations in my church are concerned, they are voluntarily given. And there is no law that bars me from sending my children to school anywhere I so wish.

PANELIST 2: Can you send your child to go and burn a mosque or kill?

PASTOR GATARI: I've never told the son of anyone to do that. But my son reserves the right to defend his land and his right to worship his Lord.

(*Lights out.*)

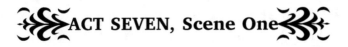

ACT SEVEN, Scene One

Interrogation room. The three panelists interrogate two policemen.

PANELIST 2: What are your ranks?

POLICEMAN 1: I'm a sergeant.

POLICEMAN 2: I'm an inspector.

PANELIST 2: You shot and killed an innocent man at a checkpoint when you were on duty last week?

POLICEMAN 1: The man approached the checkpoint. He was supposed to stop for routine check like other motorists did. He refused and drove fast.

PANELIST 2: Why then did you not chase him to arrest him instead of killing him?

POLICEMAN 1: We didn't have a functional vehicle to chase him.

PANELIST 2: And then you made it up by killing him?

POLICEMAN 1: I actually aimed at his thigh but before then I fired a warning shot in the air and he refused to stop. And people like that who refuse to stop are mostly criminals or terrorists intending to do harm.

PANELIST 3: And the best thing to do is to kill him?

POLICEMAN 1: Sir, if he was allowed, he could do a lot of harm.

PANELIST 1: You killed him and nothing was found in his car.

POLICEMAN 1: Sir, a gun was found in his car.

PANELIST 1: Which you planted to justify your action.

POLICEMAN 1: Not at all, Sir. It was his gun.

PANELIST 1: You are accused of extorting motorists.

POLICEMAN 1: Never, Sir.

PANELIST 1: When you were arrested, a lot of money was found in your pocket.

POLICEMAN 1: Sir, they voluntarily give. And I never extorted.

PANELIST 2: DPO.

POLICEMAN 2: Sir.

PANELIST 2: You ordered your men daily to raid people's homes and make arrests, then you detain and collect money for bail to set them free.

POLICEMAN 2: No, Sir. What we do is that anytime we have information about any criminal activities going on or about to happen, I immediately dispatch my men to make arrest in order to forestall such a crime.

PANELIST 2: And to let go, they have to pay for bail?

POLICEMAN 2: Sir, bail is free. We never force anyone to give money.

PANELIST 2: But when they give 'voluntarily', you collect?

POLICEMAN 2: Sometimes detainees just decide to give on their own as a contribution for maintenance of their toilets. And if we need to buy stationeries.

PANELIST 2: Don't you get imprest for maintenance and your stationeries? Must you extort from detainees?

POLICEMAN 2: Sir, you need to come and see the way we work. My station is desolate. No communication equipment, no regular power supply, no regular pipe-borne water. And the cells are congested.

PANELIST 3: Where do you live?

POLICEMAN 2: I live in a one bedroom apartment in the police barracks. I share a room and a parlour with my seven children.

PANELIST 3: But we have report that you are building a big castle in your village. And there is a report indicting you for selling and hiring weapons to armed criminals.

POLICEMAN 2: That is a wild allegation. The house in view belongs to my wife. And she's been building it for long. And I have never hired out or sold any weapon to any criminal. But it's their way of incriminating police officers and tarnishing their image for fighting them.

PANELIST 3: We have a report that said late last year, a wealthy man approached you to arrest a man with which he was sharing the same woman and you did. And you were paid.

POLICEMAN 2: The man you referred to as wealthy just came to our station and filed a complaint of breach of trust and we acted.

PANELIST 3: But you tortured the detainee.

POLICEMAN 2: We just tried to get more information from him.

PANELIST 3: And you stripped him naked. Used a cable to beat him. And insisted that he confesses.

POLICEMAN 2: No, Sir. He was trying to fault the investigating police officer. He was being rude.

PANELIST 3: You supply Indian hemp to your detainees.

POLICEMAN 2: Not at all, Sir, we can never do such a thing.

PANELIST 3: But during our unscheduled inspection of your cells, we found Indian hemp in the pockets of most of your detainees.

POLICEMAN 2: Sir, you know these people are criminals. Their family and friends sometimes have a way of beating our security system by concealing Indian hemp in the food they bring to them in the cells.

PANELIST 3: But I thought you inspect every item before you pass it on.

POLICEMAN 2: Yes, we do but sometimes they beat our intelligence.

PANELIST 2: We learnt you allow them to use Indian hemp and the leaders of the detainees contribute money for you.

POLICEMAN 2: That's not true, Sir.

PANELIST 2: In the month of February, your men raided a house, molested a woman and her child and picked seven young adults, brought them to your station, detained them, took them out at midnight and in the morning you lined up their corpses.

POLICEMAN 2: Sir, those young men were fanatics. They were criminals. Yes, we took them out for investigation and they tried to escape.

PANELIST 2: And you killed them?

POLICEMAN 2: They were very dangerous people. They wanted to harm our men.

PANELIST 2: How can armless men in your custody and in handcuffs be of any harm to your men?

POLICEMAN 2: They preached violence and hatred and had been killing people.

PANELIST 1: You succeeded in arresting them. And you did not see the value of taking them to court. So you killed them. Is that what you are trained to do?

POLICEMAN 2: Sir, my job is to enforce the law. Those persons were criminals. We found sophisticated arms and ammunitions in their custody. We cannot be blamed for not doing our job if our society will continue to treat these criminals with kid gloves.

PANELIST 1: There are legal ways to process a criminal. What you did is not legal. You will have to defend yourself and your career is at risk. Extrajudicial murders have become your lot. You are the police but you are not the state. You are paid by the tax-payers. You must learn to respect the law. You will pay for your recklessness.

(Lights out.)

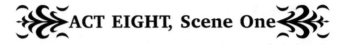# ACT EIGHT, Scene One

At the community centre, we see women and youths who are summoned by TANI *and* MARTHA *to speak for peace.*

TANI: (*Stands at the centre of the gathering.*) We gather here as mothers, wives and victims. We are here to salvage our once peaceful and united town which is now a theatre of violence. (*Crowd cheers.*)

MARTHA: (*Stands beside* TANI.) We are here as a people against violence, terror, intolerance and divisive mischief. (*Crowd cheers.*)

TANI: We are here as Muslims and Christians standing up against extremism and hatred. Today we will march to recover our freedom, our rights and our unity stolen. (*Crowd cheers.*)

MARTHA: Today, we will march to defy violence, defy gunmen, defy bombs, defy security agents who are exploiting the situation to violate our fundamental rights. (*Crowd cheers.*)

TANI: This violence and terror has consumed our children, our brothers, our sisters and our lives. This is the time to end silence and fear, this is the time to defend our rights, our liberty and our unity! (*Crowd cheers.*)

MARTHA: Christians and Muslims are one. We worship one God and have lived in the same town for generations. We must all say no to hatred and intolerance. (*Crowd cheers.*)

TANI: The politicians, the traditional rulers, the clerics have all taken to silence or complicity while our town is burning. We stand here together as one to clearly and loudly say no to violence! (*Crowd cheers.*)

MARTHA: This is a message to gunmen and bombers that you can shoot and you can bomb but you cannot break our spirit and our soul. (*Crowd cheers.*)

TANI: This is a message to those who cherish violence that you cannot take our freedom nor can you break our resolve for justice and unity. (*Crowd cheers.*)

MARTHA: We will march through the streets and raise placards and smoke out the rodents in our midst. (*Crowd cheers.*)

TANI: We will go from house to house and flush out all those pests inimical to our peace and destructive to our unity and freedom. (*Crowd cheers.*)

MARTHA: We will not tolerate or accommodate bombers in our midst. We will not accommodate or tolerate security agents molesting, maiming and humiliating us. (*Crowd cheers.*)

TANI: We will chase them out today and defend our mosques, our churches, our schools, our markets and our homes. This is a propitious cause. Move! Move!! Move!!!

(*Ructions as a phalanx raises placards reading 'no to violence', 'no to terror', 'no to intolerance', 'we are one', 'we are the people'. The crowd sweeps streets and homes parading politicians, clerics, bombers and gunmen in handcuffs.*)

Kraftgriots

Also in the series (DRAMA) *(continued)*

Emmanuel Emasealu: *The Gardeners* (2008)
Emmanuel Emasealu (ed.) *The CRAB Plays I* (2008)
Emmanuel Emasealu (ed.) *The CRAB Plays II* (2008)
Richard Ovuorho: *Reaping the Whirlwind* (2008)
Sam Ukala: *Two plays* (2008)
Ahmed Yerima: *Akuabata* (2008)
Ahmed Yerima: *Tuti* (2008)
Niyi Adebanjo: *Two Plays: A Market of Betrayals & A Monologue on the Dunghill* (2008)
Chris Anyokwu: *Homecoming* (2008)
Ahmed Yerima: *Mojagbe* (2009)
Ahmed Yerima: *The Ife Quartet* (2009)
'Muyiwa Ojo: *Memoirs of a Lunatic* (2009)
John Iwuh: *Spellbound* (2009)
Osita C. Ezenwanebe: *Dawn of Full Moon* (2009)
Ahmed Yerima: *Dami's Cross & Atika's Well* (2009)
Osita C. Ezenwanebe: *Giddy Festival* (2009)
Peter Omoko: *Battles of Pleasure* (2009)
Ahmed Yerima: *Little Drops ...* (2009)
Arnold Udoka: *Long Walk to a Dream* (2009), winner, 2010 ANA/NDDC J.P. Clark drama prize
Arnold Udoka: *Inyene: A Dance Drama* (2009)
Chris Anyokwu: *Termites* (2010)
Julie Okoh: *A Haunting Past* (2010)
Arnold Udoka: *Mbarra: A Dance Drama* (2010)
Chukwuma Anyanwu: *Another Weekend, Gone!* (2010)
Oluseyi Adigun: *Omo Humuani: Abubaka Olusola Saraki, Royal Knight of Kwara* (2010)
Eni Jologho Umuko: *The Scent of Crude Oil* (2010)
Olu Obafemi: *Ogidi Mandate* (2010), winner, 2011 ANA/NDDC J.P. Clark drama prize
Ahmed Yerima: *Ajagunmale* (2010)
Ben Binebai: *Drums of the Delta* (2010)
'Diran Ademiju-Bepo: *Rape of the Last Sultan* (2010)
Chris Iyimoga: *Son of a Chief* (2010)
Arnold Udoka: *Rainbow Over the Niger & Nigeriana* (2010)
Julie Okoh: *Our Wife Forever* (2010)
Barclays Ayakoroma: *A Matter of Honour* (2010)
Barclays Ayakoroma: *Dance on His Grave* (2010)
Isiaka Aliagan: *Olubu* (2010)
Ahmed Yerima: *Mu'adhin's Call* (2011)
Emmanuel Emasealu: *Nerves* (2011)

Alex Roy-Omoni: *The Ugly Ones* (2011)
Osita Ezenwanebe: *Adaugo* (2011)
Osita Ezenwanebe: *Daring Destiny* (2011)
Ahmed Yerima: *No Pennies for Mama* (2011)
Ahmed Yerima: *Mu'adhin's Call* (2011)
Barclays Ayakoroma: *A Chance to Survive and Other Plays* (2011)
Barclays Ayakoroma: *Castles in the Air* (2011)
Arnold Udoka: *Akon* (2011)
Arnold Udoka: *Still Another Night* (2011)
Sunnie Ododo: *Hard Choice* (2011)
Sam Ukala: *Akpakaland and Other Plays* (2011)
Greg Mbajiorgu: *Wake Up Everyone!* (2011)
Ahmed Yerima: *Three Plays* (2011)
Ahmed Yerima: *Igatibi* (2012)
Esanmabeke Opuofeni: *Song of the Gods* (2012)
Karo Okokoh: *Teardrops of the Gods* (2012)
Esanmabeke Opuofeni: *The Burning House* (2012)
Dan Omatsola: *Olukume* (2012)
Alex Roy-Omoni: *Morontonu* (2012)
Dauda Enna: *Banquet of Treachery* (2012)
Chinyere G. Okafor: *New Toyi-Toyi* (2012)
Greg Mbajiorgu: *The Prime Minister's Son* (2012)
Karo Okokoh: *Sunset So Soon* (2012)
Sunnie Ododo: *Two Liberetti: To Return from the Void & Vanishing Vapour*
   (2012)